THE WISDOM OF THE SUFIS

THE AUTHOR

*Kenneth Cragg was born in Blackpool. He grad-
uated from Oxford where he won University prizes
in Divinity and Moral Philosophy. He returned
there to read for his doctorate. He taught in the
University of Beirut and was Assistant Bishop in
the Middle East. He has travelled widely in all the
Arab countries, lectured in Muslim Universities
and taught in the USA. He has been Warden of
St Augustine's College, Canterbury, Bye-Fellow of
Gonville & Caius College, Cambridge, and has held
professorships at Hartford Theological Seminary,
University of Ibadan, Nigeria and Union Theological Seminary, New York. He is now Reader
in Religious Studies in the University of Sussex
and Assistant Bishop in the Diocese of Chichester.
Dr Cragg is the author of many books including*
The Call of the Minaret, Sandals at the Mosque,
The House of Islam, The Event of the Qur'an,
and The Mind of the Qur'an.

THE WISDOM OF
THE SUFIS

COMPILED
BY KENNETH CRAGG

A NEW DIRECTIONS BOOK

ACKNOWLEDGMENTS

Some of the translations in this volume have been selected from
previously published books. Grateful acknowledgment is made to
the following publishers for permission to reprint: Cambridge University Press, for *The Cambridge History of Islam*, edited by P. M.
Holt, *et al.*; Orientalia, Inc., for *Love of God, A Sufic Approach*,
by Mir Valiuddin; John Murray, Ltd., London, for *The Invoca-
tions of Ansari of Herat*, translated by Jogendra Singh; Perennial
Books, London, for *Letters of a Sufi Master*, translated by Titus
Burckhardt; The University of Michigan Press, for *Aspects of
Islamic Civilization*, by A. J. Arberry.

Manufactured in the United States of America
First published clothbound and as New Directions Paperbook 424
in 1976 by arrangement with Sheldon Press, London

Library of Congress Cataloging in Publication Data
Main entry under title:

The Wisdom of the Sufis.

(A New Directions Book)
1. Sufism—Quotations.   I. Cragg, Kenneth.
BP189.62.W57   297'.4   76–7032
ISBN 0–8112–0626–2
ISBN 0–8112–0627–0 pbk.

New Directions Books are published for James Laughlin
by New Directions Publishing Corporation,
333 Sixth Avenue, New York 10014

THE WISDOM OF THE SUFIS

I do not know the man so bold
He dare in lonely place
That awful stranger—consciousness
Deliberately face.

YET the will to do so is much less daunting if the
place, the human scene, is not believed to be
'lonely', but, rather, somehow responsive and re-
ciprocal in an ultimate sense. The wisdom of the Sufis
lies in finding out the loneliness of the egotistical self
and attaining the community of the essential self.
Their report of that discovery is not without conflicts
of interpretation. These must be left to speak for
themselves. What matters is the consensus of their
wisdom.

In the Qur'an of Islam, the Scripture with which
Muslim mysticism, no less than Islamic orthodoxy,
belongs, there is an often quoted verse. All the
generations of humanity are heard responding to a
divine question: 'Am I not your Lord?' with the
sure affirmative: 'Yes! indeed. We acknowledge it.'
(Surah 7.172.) In that brief exchange is summarized all
the fervour, the poetry, the discipline, the subtlety of
Sufism and its themes. The mutual love of God and
man is the single ground of all its forms, in a rich, if
sometimes sharp, diversity of awareness and experience. The meaning of this Quranic verse is that the

human of every generation, even before it is born and housed in the flesh, is pledged to a God relationship which is its deepest mystery and secret.

Sufi poets and saints have loved to cite this passage as the text of their discipleship. It states both the vision and the impulse within their search for reality. One of the sweetest of their writers, Ibn al-Farid, who lived in Cairo in the early thirteenth century, wove the words into his master poem. 'Verily Thou art the desire of my heart, the end of my search, the goal of my aim, my choice and my chosen.'

Such ardour, however, as he well knew, having travelled the road, has much to learn. Such lyrical loving may be no more than self love in disguise. For, as James Joyce cynically observed elsewhere: 'Love loves to love love,' and may be the most selfish of the self's deceits, a sheer lust for possession. There is a path of purging to be taken if authentic love is to dwell in a true self. Some commentators on Surah 7.172 suggest a hint of this in an intriguing play on words they have detected. The Arabic 'Yea!' men say to God spells adversity as well as affirmation. In the very assenting, trouble comes. There is a long, hard way for the real self to the real Lord. From the beginning, the world's and our own, truth and travail, trust and test, life and sorrow, have gone hand in hand. The pact with God is no instant peace, but a radical refining.

So the Sufi masters learned and taught. Their struggle and their benediction took shape in a wealth

4

of forms and orders, of disciplines and devotion, bringing self to Self, the soul to its Lord. Ibn al-Farid hears the voice that both rebukes and invites.

Thou art sworn to love, but to love of self, witness the fact that thou sufferest one of thy attributes to remain in existence. For thou lovest me not, so long as thou hast not passed away in me: and thou hast not passed away so long as my form is not seen within thee. . . . Such is love: unless thou die, thou wilt not win thy will of the Beloved in aught. Then choose death or leave my love alone.

The same yearning for a truth of being, where the soul is lost in its proper music, breathes through Jalal al-Din Rumi's famous 'Song of the Reed', which opens his *Mathnawi*, a vast treasure house of poetical devotion in the Persian tongue and the Sufi tradition.

Hearken to this reed forlorn,
Breathing ever since 'twas torn
From its rushy bed a strain
Of impassioned love and pain.

The secret of my song, though near,
None can see and none can hear.
O for a friend to know the sign
And mingle all his soul with mine.

'Tis the flame of love that fired me:
'Tis the wine of love inspired me.
Would'st thou learn how lovers bleed?
Hearken, hearken to the reed.

5

'A friend to know the sign' neatly phrases the intention of this short, annotated anthology of Islamic Sufism. There are several such in existence. For mysticism has a perennial fascination, not least in these times of western self-questioning and puzzled dismay about the patterns and frustrations of contemporary history. The selection that follows has been determined by a desire to relate Islamic mysticism fairly to the total context of Muslim faith and life. In some hands, Sufism emerges as a fund of anecdotes about odd characters with uncanny intelligence and pithy wit and a quaint facility for administering commendable admonition, often regaled with lively tricks of moral education. This sort of sanctified commonsense, amusing, cajoling, instructing, satirizing, a perversely foolish humanity, has its due appeal, provided we do not imagine that this prolific anecdotage tells the whole significance of the Sufis! At least it makes a pleasant prelude to them.

A certain man was believed to have died and was being prepared for burial, when he revived. He sat up, but was so shocked at the scene around him that he fainted. He was put in a coffin and the funeral party set off for the cemetery. Just as they arrived at the grave, he regained consciousness, lifted the coffin lid and cried out for help. 'It is not possible that he has revived,' said the mourners, 'because he was certified dead by competent experts'. 'But I am alive,' shouted the man. He appealed to a well-

6

known and impartial scientist and jurisprudent who was present. 'Just a moment,' said the expert. He then turned to the mourners, counting them. 'Now we have heard what the alleged deceased has had to say. You fifty witnesses tell me what you regard as the truth.' 'He is dead,' said the witnesses. 'Bury him,' said the expert. And so he was buried.

Life sometimes has no chance against entrenched authority, scholastic and ecclesiastical.

Another story illustrates the purist temptations of doctrine.

Moses once heard a shepherd praying as follows:

'O God, show me where Thou art, that I may become Thy servant. I will clean Thy shoes, and comb Thy hair and sew Thy clothes and fetch Thee milk.'

When Moses heard him praying thus in a senseless manner, he rebuked him saying: 'O foolish one, though your father was a Muslim you have become an infidel. God is Spirit and needs not such gross ministrations as, in your ignorance, you suppose.'

The shepherd was abashed at his rebuke and tore his clothes and fled into the desert. Then a voice from heaven was heard saying: 'O Moses, wherefore have you driven away my servant? Your office is to reconcile my people with me, not to drive them away from me.'

7

Though Moses is rebuked, the story at least allows him a certain satisfaction in being sophisticated. Uncouth ideas reach heaven all right. But the mystic with his superior knowledge is not among those who hold them. It was an easy step to go further and assume, as some Sufis did, that even discerning theology was really no better than the shepherd's crudity, once the ecstatic truth has been attained. But this is to anticipate.

There is an underlying irony in most religious situations. A man, say the Sufis, was surprised to find the devil was wise and handsome, not hideous and ugly as he had been led to think. 'My friend,' said the devil, 'you have been listening to my detractors!'

Something of the enigmatic quality of the true mystic comes in stories like the following:

In one of the great court banquets, everyone was seated according to rank, awaiting the entry of the King. In came a plain, shabby man and took a seat above everyone else. His boldness angered the prime minister, who ordered the newcomer to identify himself. Was he a minister? No. More. Was he the King? No, above him. Was he then the Prophet? No. More. 'Are you then God?' asked the prime minister. 'I am beyond that also,' replied the poor man. 'There is nothing beyond God,' retorted the prime minister. 'That nothing,' came the response, 'is me.'

Delectable as these stories are and saleable as

current anthologies prove—real mysticism in Islam is more than these and demands more of the student.

There are other connoisseurs who tend to lose themselves in intricate theosophy, presenting Sufism as an elaborate, esoteric system of abstract ideas, the form of which almost fatally overstrains the Islamic moorings to which it is tied. The range of Quranic vocabulary and idiom, although wide and flexible, is then unduly taxed with the meanings given to it. With such interpreters, the very confession of the divine transcendence is liable to be read in a sense which, in any recognizable Islamic terms, comes close to its denial. An intolerable tension is then set up between Islam and the more wayward mystics. The gist, though by no means all the subtleties, of this situation will be evident in the extracts which follow.

It is on this account that some expositors have seen Sufism as an import from outside into the mainstream of Islam. Among external factors would be the Christian asceticism met in conquered territories, and influences from Asian Hinduism mediated first through Persia in the early centuries and physically encountered later when Mahmud of Ghaznā and then Babur carried Islam beyond Sind into the heart of India. There were also ideas from Greek Neo-Platonism, filtered through varied, uncertainly identifiable, channels into the Islamic stream of mind and spirit.

Such external factors were undoubtedly present and Sufism is not to be understood without them. But it would be false to overlook the elements in Sufism that are native to Muslim genius and to Islamic religion. From some angles, it is true, Islam would seem the least likely soil from which mysticism should spring, so severe and uncompromising is its theological dogma. Its sense of the Qur'an is direct and clear as a book mediated from heaven in which 'there is nothing dubious'. Its prophet is firmly understood to be entirely human, an instrument or mouthpiece, recruiting in a language given in the name of God—the God of transcendent majesty, altogether other than man, exalted in highest glory. Islamic theology, in orthodox hands, brooks no compromise of its confident theism —the sort of compromise which is never far away from the instincts of mysticism. Asian views of reality and of intuitive knowledge, with all their elusiveness, would seem quite uncongenial to the soil of positive Islam, in no way likely to take root there and to flourish.

Yet, clearly, they did take root, and not only by external seeding. Though the reasons may be paradoxical, the Muslim soil brought them to a harvest. Among the interior factors were those which also contributed to the emergence of the basic division of Islam into the Sunni and the Shi'ah elements. These were, in part, political disappointment with events and government, which produced sectarian, or mystical, dissociation from prevailing patterns. Within these political factors, were more deeply lying psychic and religious causes which created an urge towards mystical satisfactions, for which belief and cult supplied inner meanings beneath their outer forms. The Qur'an itself could be seen as possessing a hidden mystique of language below its surface text, while its prophet might be claimed as the supreme Sufi, having his message by an ecstasy of experience, as light in which his Sufi disciples might bask.

Even the clear assertion of God's supremacy, found in orthodox doctrine, which seemed to account for all mystery, could nevertheless be interpreted in a mystical sense. The divine lordship extended over all causes and events, presiding over the smallest details of human will and deed. Divine decree covered all things. One only had to think of that omnipresent reality as an ocean rather than a throne, as pervasive light rather than a single sun above, to have passed from rigorous monotheism to the characteristic Sufi meaning of an identity between each and all and the One. To sustain that central theme of mystical absorption it was possible to claim with confidence a variety of Quranic texts. (Cf. No. LXXII.)

All these interior factors, deriving from the theology, the prophethood, the scripture, of Islam itself, lay within the growth of Sufism, responding, as it certainly was, to the stimulus or the contagion of the cultures with which Islam was involved in the centuries that followed the initial period (about a single century) during which the Arabic language became the effective organ of exchange throughout the vast dispersion of the faith.

There is no place here to explore the fascinating

questions that concern the historian and the theologian in this field. The aim is to savour those writers who in prose and verse expressed the Sufi genius and its awareness of 'the self and the Lord'. We read in them the living commentary on the primary question of Surah 7.172 with which we began.

'Am I not your Lord?' The question addresses man universally. In our individuality it confronts us with ourselves. It questions our existence radically, searches the why and wherefore of our being. It invites the answer Yes! Giving the answer is the essence of human awareness. Not, as the philosopher Descartes had it: 'I think and so I am', but: 'I am and so I relate, divinely'. This truth we only rightly confess when we learn to reverse it and also say: 'I relate divinely, and so I am'. In such relating a different sort of 'I' comes into being, an 'I' that is no more independent, in the old sense no more 'I' at all.

It will be well to grasp this theme firmly. For it is the very core of Sufism. It requires us to face a kind of paradox which Jalal al-Din (whose Reed Song we have quoted earlier) sweetly condensed into eight lines. If, at first reading, they prove puzzling, the rest of the anthology will help. But when the puzzle ceases to be one, Sufism has become an open secret.

> Awhile, as wont may be,
> Self I did claim:
> True self I did not see
> But heard its name.

I, being self-confined,
Self did not merit,
Till, leaving self behind,
Did self inherit.

'Self I did claim.' That is where we all start. It is the
instinctive posture of life. Self and self-consciousness
seem to be, simply, an equation. But, the Sufis find and
teach, this self-centred selfhood is illusory: it only
hints at a possibility it quite fails to attain as long as it
is thought of as self-sufficient. 'True self I did not see.'
While, in attitude and assumption, I am 'confined
to self', personality remains unrealized. Such self-
centred selfhood has to be left behind: only so does a
true selfhood come to be. We have to lose in order to
find.

Accordingly, with this clue in mind, we explore the
mystics in four sequences. All their history and their
manifold literature may be learned dependably by
this road. They are: Me—the self; Thou—the Lord;
We—the unity; 'Lord of the worlds'.

The fourth heading, a quotation from the Qur'an
and Muslim prayer, is vital, for reasons which will
appear below. It properly issues, for many though
not all Sufis, from the sequence of the other three.

'I,' 'Thou,' and 'We' might be said to stand, in this
outline, for the task, the search, and the goal, of the
mystic. The pronouns, it must be agreed, are suspect,
if they suggest notions of separation and apartness. For
these, Sufis are set to deny and escape. 'In his divine

13

majesty,' wrote one of them, ' "I", "Thou", and "We" shall not be found. "I", "Thou", "We", and "He", bear the same meaning. For in unity there is no division. Every man who has annihilated the body hears within his heart a voice that cries: "I am God".'

Yet even such a writer continues to use pronouns and to speak of encounter. All are at least agreed that, whether or not religious experiences ceases to be that of a subject and an object, it starts there. Each of us begins, 'as wont may be', with 'me', with 'things of weight that task our thoughts', as Shakespeare puts it. We start with the necessity, the burden, the enigma of being the selves we are. The self, its nature and meaning, are precisely the self's problem. Even the suicide, extinguishing the self, is radically being one.

How then is selfhood as the ground of 'me' saved from selfishness as the blight and curse of 'me'? What does one do with the ego-existent in order to escape the ego-enemy? Or are these questions themselves incomplete, because they still cling to an individual identity that, somehow, has to be transcended?

The Sufis, especially the earliest among them, understood the self in line with three Quranic terms describing it. These have entered deeply into Islamic psychology. They are: 'the soul biased to evil', 'the soul aware that it is in the wrong', and 'the soul attaining to peace'. The first, *al-nafs al-ammarah*, occurs in the story of Joseph and Pharaoh's officer's wife, Zulaikha by name, who tried to seduce him when he served in

14

her husband's household. Joseph mastered the tempta-
tion. But he acknowledged how Zulaikha's infatu-
ation with his beauty had constituted a sharp test in
which he had to struggle against an innate consent to
the evil (Surah 12.53). Like all human souls, he felt
himself under a compulsion to desire. This is the sense
of the word *ammarah*, meaning an inner command
predisposing us to the evil and the false. We register
the right but incline to the wrong. Let us call it
—though with some reduction of emphasis—'the
problematic self'.

This awareness of the soul's bias leads to self-
accusation, to *al-nafs al-lawwamah* (Surah 75.2). This
is 'the inauthentic self', the self that knows its own
falsehood and so yearns for true being beyond the
false. It suffers from what the mystics called 'the
wound of absence'. Its sense of reproach is the gate of
hope. To take the inauthentic for all there is, or, still
more, not to know it inauthentic, is to be altogether
undone. Only out of accusation can there come ex-
pectancy. Self-blame is the way into the third condi-
tion, *al-nafs al-mutma'innah* (Surah 89.27), 'the soul
attaining to peace'. Out of un-ease, through existential
disquiet, into soul-peace in God—such is the Sufi path.
The tranquillity of the soul in peace comes only through
the travail of the soul dismayed.

We have, then, to discover first the deep, mystical
literature of penitence and contrition. Much of this is
found in devotional manuals, known as *aurad*, which
the various Orders of Sufism received from their

15

founders in the twelfth century and after. This is an area which some anthologies neglect. The great masters of soul searching, however, belong to the earliest days of Sufism when, in protest against moral compromise, many writers reflected on the sickness of the human spirit. To follow this route into Islamic wisdom is also to coincide with historical sequence. The inauthentic self is the point of departure, the man I am, as the only prelude to the man I might become. This dimension of Sufism is the theme of sayings I to LIII.

It demanded the path of self-examination and re-proach, willingly entered and patiently pursued. The way is marked by a succession of stages, or stations, each registered and rewarded by corresponding states of heart. Beginning with repentance and abnegation, the soul passed through the long road of dispossession to absorption into God. First the disciple was 'one who desired', a *murid*, then a wayfarer of the spirit, a *salik*, and finally a sharer of the secret, a *wasil*, an initiate. To guide and test the aspirant a spiritual master was imperative. One could not well judge and scrutinize one's own progress. The literature of Sufism is full of the theme of spiritual relationship between master and seeker. This was the touchstone by which progress could be truly known and an honesty of heart more likely ensured as in the sayings LIV to LVIII.

It was for such soul-sifting and shepherding that the great Sufi Orders came into being with their prayer rites and liturgies and the authority of their spiritual founders, some of whom attained an almost legendary reputation for piety and wisdom.

Patterns of organization and of technique varied. All were centred on the practice of *dhikr*, or recollection, the intense repetition of the divine Name *Allahu, Allahu, Allahu,* other formulas like the *Allahu akbar* of orthodox confession 'God is greater', or the Muslim creed itself *La ilaha illa Allah,* 'there is no god but God', with its liquid 'l' consonants and its repeated 'a' vowels. Such sustained recital served to bring on a state of trance and could be accompanied by rhythmic movements of the body or, in some Orders, by the flute or whirling dance.

But these were always for the sake of that inner focus of will notably expressed in the girdle liturgy of a prominent Turkish Order, the Bektashis, who, on donning the girdle (which had a seven-pointed star hanging from it), rehearsed their seven-pointed liturgy.

I tie up greediness and unbind generosity.
I tie up anger and unbind meekness.
I tie up avarice and unbind piety.
I tie up ignorance and unbind the fear of God.
I tie up passion and unbind the love of God.
I tie up hunger and unbind contentment.
I tie up the power of Satan and unbind divineness.

Thus the seeker might hope to become the traveller, the traveller the initiate, and the initiate the ecstatic.

This spiritual regimen was followed, for the most

17

part, in the open world of daily affairs. It was rare, though not unknown, for Sufi brotherhoods to withdraw altogether into monastic retreat from society. There were fraternities with lay vows of discipline. But Sufi groups were often closely knit to trading guilds and common crafts.

The stages and states of the mystic's journey to the real were told in a rich language of metaphor; hence the wealth and elusiveness of Sufi poetry. Saint and lyricist were never far apart. Metaphor is part of the very essence of the mystical mind. For logic and rational discourse cannot avail for the expression of truth. The phenomenal world is no more than a bridge to the real. As such, it cannot yield arguments from experiment but only analogies by which we move across the bridge to what lies beyond and, thus, in the end escape from it. The metaphor of sleep serves in something of the same sense as that of the bridge. For in sleep we pass away from the observable world and, being released from its preoccupations, we dwell elsewhere.

In similar vein was the much loved analogy of the veil. For the uninitiated, the real truth is veiled, but mystical experience lifts that veil to disclose the inner secret to the initiate. There are frequent allusions to this lifting of the veil in the sayings of the Sufis. Or, alternatively, the parable of wine and intoxication readily communicated a like idea. Wine symbolized the mystic rapture of love. The poet Hafiz, for example, celebrated the taverns of ecstasy where the masters, like taverners, drew their guest/disciples into truth's inward wonder.

The tavern's step shall be thy hostelry.
For love's diviner breath comes but to those
Who suppliant on that dusty threshold lie.
(See sayings XCVIII–CI.)

Most loved and suggestive of all metaphors was that of light, so tellingly used in the Qur'an itself (No. CII) in a passage every phrase of which was rich in mystical meaning as poets and seers brooded on it.

These and other fertile images pictured that state of unitive desire in which the soul attained to peace, the goal of the journey out of inauthenticity into true being in God. But that goal posed a basic question over which Sufism had a divided mind. Should that experience of union with the One, the Real, be understood as one in which the 'I' of ordinary experience no longer had any real place? Was the self essentially an illusory thing, as in the Hindu saying: 'Your very existence is your sin'? Or was the self the authentic and continuing ground of those revealing experiences of spiritual 'intoxication' which set it in true perspective?

Some mystics illustrated the question by an analogy from sunlight. When the sun is up the stars are 'out'. But they are there all the time even when 'extinguished' in the supreme light. Was mystical experience like that—the Real being the sun and selves the stars? Or was the meaning of union a unity of being, in which light was no more differentiated into

19

a great orb (the God of traditional theism) and the 'tiny' stars, a unity like the ocean which can no more be differentiated into drops though it contains innumerable drops?

Many other matters turned on this basic issue. One, for example, was the problem of language. Clearly speech is bound to use pronouns, coming from a speaker, even if he is only saying: 'I am not'. Self is so much bound up with self-consciousness and self-consciousness, of course, cannot report its own extinction. But perhaps this situation, though unavoidable, is all of one piece with the lust, pride, envy, and the like, which we can identify as 'ours' and yet will to be dispossessed of. Perhaps existence itself, as a self, is of the same order. To paraphrase an old philosopher, its being is to be denied. It exists in order that it may come not to exist. That, precisely, is what the monist forms of Sufism taught, far as their thinking strayed, in doing so, from the familiar doctrines of Islamic theology. If the chief business of existence is that it may discover it is illusory, this seems a strangely circuitous way of arranging for the discovery to be reached, since the illusion of significance, which it has to overcome, is so strong.

That, of course, among other things, was the consideration which led so many Sufis, on the other hand, to see in the state of union with God, not a final cancellation of the self, but a vocation in which it learned the illusoriness of selfishness and so found the self in truth.

We must leave the problem of language, of the 'I' negating the 'I' and of a 'Thou' being addressed which is not really separate. Perhaps mysticism can use its pronouns, 'I' 'Thou' and 'We', and yet be reporting an ecstatic oblivion in a wordless void. Language, though the Sufis loved it and wedded it to music, was, in the end, their enemy.

As well as the problem of language there is the question of nature. This is the reason why, after illustrating in quotation the state of union with God, this anthology returns, in the fourth section, to 'the Lord of the worlds'. The question of whether the self is finally illusory is bound up with the question whether nature is also illusory. For it is in relating, through the senses and desires, to the external world that the self knows itself. This has always been a dilemma for mysticism. Is the world of nature a vestibule of heaven, an ally of the spirit? Or is it a distraction, a diversion, a foe? (See below CXXXV–CLV.) Was the poet right in observing that no gold can be current without alloy? Hafiz, in his ribald and irreverent vein, asked for 'a music to which both drunk and sober might dance', pleading for an attitude to nature and to society in which the body had its place as well as the spirit its freedom. Must we spurn the candle in rejoicing in the flame? If we ascend the ladder of spirituality whose first rungs are in the senses, must these be repudiated in the heights? If we truly acknowledge 'the Lord' can the clause 'of the worlds' be detached from the confession? Will not that plural form be the right safeguard—not, merely the world, either of mundane things or of eternal mystery, but the two together and all their plural diversities of sense, and thought, and value, and reality?

As well as nature, here there is history. Mystics have been much involved in tension at this point. Some Sufis, like the fervently pious elsewhere, were liable to maximize inward evil—pride, self-will, passion—and minimize the dark social implications of wrong in the structures of human culture. An intensity of personal penitence needs also to learn how to bring society to repentance, how to generate a corporate humility, as well as a private one, a humility which would bring down the pride of nations, the arrogance of commerce, the boastings of advertisement and 'the insolence of office'. The will to purity of heart and tenderness of spirit has much business with human society around as well as with the hidden man within.

To take the self as illusory, and to seek escape from the illusion, still leaves us with the bigness of the human scene, with society beyond the person. How is the teeming, suffering world to be seen within the mystic quest? Some Sufis fell back on familiar attitudes and refrained from questioning omnipotence. A fifteenth-century Afghani Sufi from Herat wrote:

> We all but playthings be
> Of God's omnipotence:
> All might, all wealth, is He,
> We beggars without pence.

Dost thou suppose
I do as I command?
Or, as the moment goes,
I am in my own hand?

As a pen I lie
Before my scrivener:
Or like a ball am I,
My mallet's prisoner.

The third stanza has a kinship with Umar al-Khay-
yam's:

The ball no question makes of Ayes or Noes,
But here or there as strikes the player goes.
And He that tossed you down the field
He knows about it all, He knows.

Jalal al-Din Rumi varies the gambling metaphor with
a scribal one, and expresses a frequent mystical posture
in respect of history and evil: distinctions do not hold.

The power of the artist is shown by his ability to
make both the ugly and the beautiful. . . . Evil hurts
him not. To make the evil denotes in him perfection.

In any event, Rumi goes on: 'The ugliness of the
script is not the ugliness of the divine scribe.'
Mysticism is more ready for this logic than an alert
theology, though mystical practice is often better than
the theory. Yet the logic is strange. Ugliness in the
script is not ugliness in the scribe. But it is certainly

ugliness in the scribing and, as such, vital. It is precisely scribing as the clue to the scribe which mystical language about divine love necessarily affirms. For love means that the doer is known in the deed. In love there can be no escape into irresponsibility. If we take seriously the central mystical reality of love, we cannot be content with notions of power that consist merely in the ability to be arbitrary. Love itself is wanting, if the human tragedy is excluded from the bliss of desire for unity with God. The issue is too large to be resolved here. Sufism is at least close enough to reality to leave us with the question open.

Keeping in mind these issues of language, nature, history and evil, which belong with mysticism, it is necessary to look more closely at the mind of Sufism about that unity of desire in which they arise. Al-Junaid, of Baghdad, for example (d. 910), saw unity in four successive kinds. There was the belief of ordinary people that God is One, a belief which rejects all partners with God, all likenesses or equals. But such ordinary believers have hopes and fears which assume the reality of forces and agencies other than God. So while they confess the unity, they do not live it.

In the second place come the formal theologians, who both assert the divine unity and who deny, in their external acts, all alternatives to the divine authority. But inwardly, they are still egoist. The third kind both assert the unity and allow it in their inner attitudes as well as their outward behaviour. But individuality is still present.

The fourth and ultimate unity means existence beyond individuality. There is no longer God's call consciously heard and the self's answer consciously given. Man is lost to will and sense and action, and is no more himself. He is lost in God who wills, works and creates in him. This is Al-Junaid's interpretation of the meaning of Surah 7.172, with which we began. Even moral commands and prohibitions are here transcended, since these relate to humanity outside the unitive state. Yet, since they are inwardly fulfilled, the divine possession of the self, being beyond them, nevertheless achieves them through love, without their being consciously required of the will at all. Man is, moreover, called to return from this experience to normal existence, there to demonstrate divine graces. (See below CVI–CVII.)

Here the issue of the place of nature is left in characteristic ambiguity. The visual world, and also the arts of music and of colour that spring from it, are, from one angle, a blessing, from another, they mean homesickness, in that they remind of absence from unity. Or, as Rumi has it:

My praise dispraises Thee, Almighty God,
For praise is being, and to be is sin.

The Sufi here seems in need of a more forthright sense of the natural order as able, through gratitude and worship within it, to bring about that very proximity

25

to God which requires that we leave the world behind. Al-Junaid showed himself well aware of this.

It must be remembered that Al-Junaid sees the question of Surah 7.172, as being addressed to embryonic humanity, and so not yet individualized. So the answer was not theirs individually in a way that would hinge on their knowledge of the world of sense. They were not creatures, acknowledging the wonder and glory of creation, when they said: 'Yes! we own you are our lord.' The exchange of question and answer was a discourse within pure spirituality. There was no duality. Whatever answer the question has when we have become individuals, we must go back to that pure state before the veil of nature came between.

The poet of Cairo, Ibn al-Farid (d. 1234), summed up the issue most truly when he wrote:

Neither do created things veil the mystic from God, nor does God veil him from created things. Rather God reveals Himself to the mystic in both His aspects at once, so that he sees with the bodily eye the beauty of the divine essence manifested under the attribute of externality.

This was because Ibn al-Farid drew his conclusion, among other things, from a much quoted verse of the Qur'an: 'God close confines and wide outspreads . . .' (Surah 2.245). The two verbs have no stated objects but the divine grace, or bounty, is understood. They relate, according to the poet, to the normal and the

ecstatic selfhood, the limited encounter with the divine
perceptible in nature and the overwhelming intimacy
of mystical union. (See below CXXXIII.)

An important Indian Muslim mystic, Al-Sirhindi
(d. 1624), developing the familiar metaphor of wine
and ecstasy, wrote of the ultimate ecstasy, however,
as an ultimate 'sobriety'. His progression of thought
was not unlike that of Al-Junaid, from commonplace
belief to ecstatic union. In such union, man knows
God beyond creatorship, inside a secret which is above
creaturehood and has no need for the evidences of the
created order. However, this vision, though beyond
the creator/creature relationship, endorses it and calls
man to a continuing worship such as would belong
with it. Ecstasy, in other words, is an interim experience. It is falsely understood if a unity of being with
God is claimed for it. But we cannot reach the ultimate
sobriety of true worship unless we have been through
ecstasy. Only such experience, constantly renewed,
quickens us to worship beyond the self-centredness of
mere thanks-giving or petition. Or, to revert to our
earlier metaphor (which we owed to Al-Sirhindi),
the sun of intoxication and the stars of creatureliness
somehow shine simultaneously.

However various Sufis have left this issue, all are
agreed, in the words of one of them 'in a manner,
We united are'. In love's encounter, all is One and One
is all. We cannot require of the lovers an orthodox,
still less a logical, consistency.

One fascinating aspect of Islamic mysticism for

which we have here no place relates to its implications for the status of Muhammad in Sufi piety. Many Sufis have seen in him an emanation of the divine wisdom. They have ranked what they call his *wilayah*, or intimacy with God, far above his *nubuwwah*, or prophethood, which had to do with the instruction of uninitiated mankind. These, however, were developments among the later sophisticates, in which the earlier moralists and ascetics were not involved. They certainly strain the traditional understanding, not only of the finality of prophethood in the divine plan but of the nature of religion itself.

The Sufis were acute critics of the institutions of religion. Throughout their wisdom there recurs the theme of the ever present dangers in forms of observance and ritual. Many held very loosely to the externals of cult and creed and code.

Such independence of mind led them, in part at least, to a hospitality between religious systems. Spirituality discerns across the frontiers of dogma that liabilities to hypocrisy are one and that sainthood is not anywhere monopolized. Forms of allegiance may be proper. But God is independent of his devotees. 'The mystic', they said, 'looks for the ocean of love and therefore cares little for the rivers and canals of prejudice and strife.'

'Lead me from the unreal to the Real' is the age-long prayer of mystics. But how do we identify either? Which direction will the leading take? It is generally assumed that the leading tends away from the finite, the transitory and the ordinary, away from the earth, to the infinite, the timeless, the eternal, the beyond. So it may be. The clues, as Sufis read them, seem to be that way. The journey to the Real is upward to trans-cendence.

Suppose, however, when we take that way, the way of escape beyond nature and history—suppose we find that the goal itself turns our journey round and home again? What if the very transcendent is found to be earth-seeking? What if that we took as fit to be transcended, because it is lowly, is truly where the glory is and meant to be embraced? Do we rightly identify the great by uncontaminated seclusion and exaltedness? Or is the great, by its nature, in love with the world? If so the lowly is transformed by the dis-covery and the eternal may dwell in the light of common day.

It is the worth of Islamic mysticism to have lived in the meaning of the divine interrogation of the human and to have wrestled with the answers. These pages take the way of that existence in wisdom with some of its surest mentors and poets. The way moves through inauthenticity into encounter, and by encounter into unity, to the goal of 'the Lord of the worlds', to the divine questioner who stakes his identity in the human recognition.

STORIES, POEMS AND SAYINGS

*

'I'—THE SELF—DESIROUS

* I *

WHAT a sorry creature is this son of Adam, who effaces the cosmos (by multiplicity of desires) until not a trace of it remains and whom the cosmos, in its turn, will obliterate until not a trace of him remains, save a faint odour which, in a little while, fades away altogether.

* II *

WHY do you make a search for my heart?
For I do not know where it is.
Tell me yourself, what is a heart?
I do not find its trace anywhere.

* III *

MY LIFE, which is not my own,
Has no asset except its sense of wonder:
Thou art the king of the realm of beauty,
I am but a helpless beggar.

* IV *

WITHOUT losing oneself one cannot behold Thee.
He who wishes to purchase Thee
Must first sell himself.

★ V ★

I AM lost to myself. I do not know what name I bear. Am I a lover or a beloved or what? I know not.

★ VI ★

MY BREAST is oppressed, my thoughts wander, I am bewildered. Lord have mercy on one whose disease is great, whose cure is impossible to him . . . whose strength lessens while his will grows stronger. Thou art his refuge and strength, his help and his healing.

★ VII ★

I HAVE lost my purpose. I am stripped of will, lacking in strength and power. . . . O my God, my soul is a ship adrift in seas of her own will, where there is no shelter from Thee save in Thee. Appoint for her, O God, in the name of God, her course and its harbour.

★ VIII ★

YOU HAVE no other God but He. He has given you being from the earth and established you in it. So ask forgiveness of Him and repent before Him. For my Lord is near to answer. (Surah 11.61)
Man was created with a restless anxiety. When evil befalls, he is impatient, and when good comes, tight-fisted. Only the prayerful, those who are steadfast in prayers, are otherwise. On *their* possessions the beggar and the outcast have an acknowledged claim. (Surah 70.19–24)
Has there ever been over man any flux of mortal

time within which he was of no importance? We
created man from a drop of sperm, making proof of
him, giving him hearing and seeing, and setting him
in the way. The question is whether he be thankful
or thankless.   (Surah 76.1–3)
They fold their breasts to hide from Him. But even
when shrouded in their garments, He knows well
their secret selves and what they disclose. He perceives
their very hearts.   (Surah 11.5)
Say: 'I take refuge with the Lord of the daybreak,
from the evil of what He has created, and from the
evil of the enveloping darkness, and from the evil of
those who bind their spells, and from the evil of the
envier and his envy'.   (Surah 113.1–5)
Say: 'I take refuge with the Lord of men, the King
of men, the God of men, from the evil of the whisper-
ing insinuator, who whispers in the hearts of men. . . .'
(Surah 114.1–5)

★ IX ★

O God, our eyes are blinded.
O pardon us. Our sins are a heavy burden.
Thou art hidden from us, though the heavens are
    filled
With Thy light which is brighter than the sun and
    moon.
Thou art hidden: yet Thou revealest our hidden
    secrets . . .
Thou art above our conceptions and descriptions.
Dust be on our heads and our similitudes of Thee.

33

⋆ X ⋆

MAN is wrapping his net around himself.

⋆ XI ⋆

BEWARE, O believers!
You may develop innumerable states of mind.
All the seventy and two heresies lurk in you.
Have a care lest, one day, they prevail over you . . .
The sellers of base gold sit smiling in their shops
Because the touchstone is not yet in their sight.

⋆ XII ⋆

AWHILE, as wont may be
Self I did claim:
True self I did not see
But heard its name.

I, being self-confined,
Self did not merit.
Till, leaving self behind,
Did self inherit.

⋆ XIII ⋆

BE JUST, confess
In love is ample
    righteousness.
The fault lies in thyself
That thou art prone to
    sin

If thou dost claim
For human lust love's
    holy name,
Then know and prove
The way is far from lust
    to love.

⋆ XIV ⋆

GOD LOVES noble shame; shame is the mark of a noble
nature. For it is shame that first alerts the sinner to
realize what is the will of God.

★ XV ★

To REMOVE mountains from their place would be easier than to remove the love of domination when it is established in the soul.

★ XVI ★

I CONFORM to what My servant thinks of Me. If he thinks what is good, then good is his: if he thinks what is evil then evil is his.

★ XVII ★

CERTAINLY all things are hidden in their opposites— gain in loss, gift in refusal, honour in humiliation, wealth in poverty, strength in weakness, abundance in restriction, rising up in falling down, life in death, victory in defeat, power in powerlessness . . . Therefore, if a man wishes to find, let him be content to lose; if he wishes a gift let him be content with refusal. He who desires honour must accept humiliation and he who desires wealth must be satisfied with poverty. Let him who wishes to be strong be content to be weak. He who wishes to be a raised up must allow himself to be cast down. He who desires life must accept death. He who wishes to conquer must be content to be powerless. . . . The servant is the servant, and the Lord is the Lord.

★ XVIII ★

LOCK the door of covetousness and open the door of

contentment. . . . What has a creature of clay to do with pride? Let him who wishes to be near God abandon all that alienates him from God.

Purify your intention . . . take heed to your intention: it is a secret bond between you and God and in it resides singlemindedness.

* XIX *

FROM the time of Adam to the resurrection people cry: The heart, the heart! And I wish that I might find someone to describe what the heart is, or how it is. But I find none. What, then, is this heart of which I hear only the name?

* XX *

LIKE thoughts in my
    mind
Thou ever dwelling art:
If Thee I would find,
I look into my heart.

I look for equity,
Which none obtains
    from me.
Against the world I cry:
The world's complaint
    am I.

* XXI *

THEY say to me:
Why all this agony?
These sobs, these tears,
These wild and pallid
    fears?

Say not that I do wrong,
So I reply.
Behold my fair
And solve your riddle
    there.

PERFECT, perfect, perfect,   Holy, holy, holy,
Thrice perfect is this love: Thrice holy in this light,
Empty, empty, empty   Meeting, meeting,
This flesh and the lusts   meeting,
   thereof.   Today with the Infinite.

★ XXIII ★

THY BEAUTY is the heart's   O lift Thy veil to me,
   shrine,   When I Thy glory see:
The spirit's food divine: Then shall I rend apart
My soul, consumed by   The garments of my
   woe,   heart.
Doth like a candle glow.

★ XXIV ★

THE PRAYERS of the sorrowful come from burning
hearts.

★ XXV ★

IF THOU hast not seen the devil, look at thyself. Be
ashamed of thy sins, confess them humbly to God,
beseech Him to pardon them and so change thy heart
that thou wilt loathe what thou hast done and re-
nounce it utterly.

★ XXVI ★

IN THE WORLD, the beginning is from the word No!
This is the first station of the man of God.

★ XXVII ★

O GOD, show us all things in this house of deception:
show them as they really are.

★ XXVIII ★

O GRACIOUS LORD, with whom disguise is vain,
Mask not our evil: let us see it plain.
But veil the weakness of our good desire,
Lest we lose heart and falter and expire.

★ XXIX ★

YOU have feet, why pretend to be lame? You have
hands, why conceal the fingers that grip?

★ XXX ★

HE WHO, by remembering Me, is distracted from his
petition, will receive more than those who ask.

★ XXXI ★

GOD SAID: O world, serve those who serve Me and
render weary those who serve you.

★ XXXII ★

O SON, did you ever present your silver body as an
offering to the damsels pictured on bath walls?

★ XXXIII ★

WITH dust my heart is thick that should be clear,
A glass to mirror forth the great King's face:
One ray of light from out Thy dwelling place
To pierce my night, O God, and draw me near.

⋆ XXXIV ⋆

LORD, Thou knowest that I am a hundred times worse than Thou hast declared. But beyond my exertion and action, beyond good and evil, faith and infidelity, beyond living righteously or behaving disobediently, I had great hope of Thy loving kindness. I turn again to that pure grace. I do not regard my own works. Thou gavest me my being as a robe of honour: I have always relied on that munificence.

⋆ XXXV ⋆

COME, O heart . . . set thy whole desire on that
  whereof thou hast no hope,
For thou hast come far from original hopelessness.
Be silent, that the Lord who gave thee language may
  speak.
For, as He fashioned a door and a lock, He also made
  a key.

⋆ XXXVI ⋆

GOD SAYS: Come, come, do not spend your life in wandering to and fro, since there is no market elsewhere for your money. You are a dry valley and I am as the rain: you are as a ruined city and I as the architect.

⋆ XXXVII ⋆

MY SERVANT never ceases to come closer to Me, through voluntary devotions, until I love him. And when I love him, I am the ear with which he hears,

39

the eye with which he sees, the hand with which he grasps.

⋆ XXXVIII ⋆

YOU know to what the soul, in its bias to evil, calls you. It was created weak: albeit its nature is strong in greed and dissimulation. For it is confident, self-assertive, disobedient to God, untrustworthy. Its sincerity consists in lying: its claims are based on vanity. All that comes from it is deceitful: nothing that it does is praiseworthy. Be not deluded by this self, its hopes and desires. For if you leave it alone you are led astray and if you give it what it desires it will perish.

⋆ XXXIX ⋆

HE who fears ought else but God is in fear of all things.

⋆ XL ⋆

CONTEMPLATION is the battle-ground of men: mortification is the playground of children.

⋆ XLI ⋆

I ASK God's forgiveness for my lack of faithfulness in asking His forgiveness.

⋆ XLII ⋆

THE SPIRITUAL AIM is reached neither by many works, nor by few, but by grace alone. As the saint Ibn 'Ata-Allah says in his counsels: If you were destined to reach Him only after the destruction of your faults and the abandonment of all your claims, you would never reach Him. . . . He absorbs your quality into His and your attributes into His and thus brings you back by means of what comes to you from Him, not by means of what comes to Him from you.

* XLIII *

Is IT NOT high time that the hearts of those who have believed should be hushed to reverence at the remembrance of God and of the truth sent down? (Surah 57.16)

* XLIV *

O THOU who art alive
By this world's breath,
Shame on thee to survive
In living death!

Then never Love forgo
Or thou shalt die:
In love expire, and so
Live deathlessly.

* XLV *

IT WAS RELATED of Sari al-Saqati of Baghdad, who had a shop in the bazaar, that when word came of a fire in which his shop was burnt, he said: Then I am set free from the care of it. Later, there came word that his shop was intact but that those around it had been destroyed. Then Sari gave all he possessed to the poor and took the way of a sufi.

* XLVI *

IT WAS RELATED of Abu Turab al-Nakhshabi, of Khurasan, that he said: My food is what I find, my

41

clothing what covers me, and my dwelling place is where I alight. He was alone in the desert when death came to him. His friends found him there, standing on his feet, his face turned towards the Qiblah of Mecca, his water-pot beside him and his staff gripped in his hand. The wild animals had left him unmolested.

★ XLVII ★

THE repentance of fear is caused by revelation of God's majesty; the repentance of shame by the vision of God's beauty.

★ XLVIII ★

OUR ALIENATION and severance from Thy beauty all proceed from ourselves. Deliver us from ourselves and grant us the intimate knowledge of Thyself.

★ XLIX ★

URGED by desire, I wandered in the streets
Of good and evil. I gained nothing except feeding the fire of desire.

★ L ★

ESSENCE is poverty—accidents, all else be.
Poverty is heart's ease
And all else the soul's disease.
The round world complete
Delusion is and deceit:
Poverty is the sole
Treasure and spirit's goal.

★ LI ★

QUIT thyself, and thou shalt attain to Me.
Of a surety, he who is annihilated in the truth
attains to the very reality of all that is.

★ LII ★

FROM realms of formlessness, existence doth take form
And fades again therein. To Him we must return.

★ LIII ★

THIS is possible only through hard striving and
earnest endeavour to expel vain thoughts and imagin-
ations from thy mind.

The more these thoughts are cast out and these
suggestions checked, the stronger and closer relation
[with thy Lord] becomes. It is, then, necessary to use
every endeavour to force these thoughts to encamp
outside the enclosure of thy breast, and that the Truth
most glorious may cast His beams into thy heart, and
deliver thee from thyself, and save thee from the
burden of entertaining His rivals in thy heart.

Then there will abide with thee neither consciousness of thyself, nor even consciousness of such
absence of consciousness—nay, there will abide nothing
save the One God alone.

What doth it profit thee to allow thyself to be
guided by vain passions and desires? Why dost thou
rely on these transitory objects that glitter with false
lustre? Turn thy heart away from them all and attach

it firmly to God. Break loose from all these and cleave closely to Him. It is only He who has always been and will ever be. The countenance of His eternity is never scarred by the thorn of contingency.

★ LIV ★

THAT NIGHT I asked God to confirm my intention (of becoming a disciple of 'Ali al-Jawal) and I spent the whole night picturing him to myself, wondering what he was like and how my meeting with him would be, unable to sleep. When morning came, I went to find him in his *zawiyah*, in the Rumaylah quarter, located between the two cities (of Fez) on the river bank, in the direction of the Qiblah, on the very spot where his tomb lies today. I knocked on the gate and there he was before me, sweeping out the *zawiyah*, as was his custom. For he never gave up sweeping it every day with his own blessed hand, in spite of his great age and high spiritual function.

What do you want? he asked. O my Lord, I replied, I want you to take me by the hand for God.

Then he began to reprove me furiously, hiding his true state from my eyes with words such as these: And who told you that I take any one at all by the hand and why ever should I do so for you? And he drove me away—all to test my sincerity.

So I went away. But when night came, I questioned God once more (by means of the Holy Book). Then, after performing the morning prayer, I went back

44

again to the *zawiyah*. I found the master, again sweeping as before, and knocked at the gate. He opened it and let me in and I said: Take me by the hand for God's sake.

Then he took me by the hand and said: 'Welcome!' He led me into his dwelling place in the inner part of the *zawiyah* and manifested great joy. 'O my Lord,' I said to him, 'I have been looking for a master for so long.' 'And I,' he replied, 'was looking for a sincere disciple.'

* LV *

THE DERVISH an' he
   disclose
The world's great
   mystery,
Each moment he bestows
A royal realm on thee.

He is no dervish true
That meanly begs for
   bread,
But raises up anew
The living from the
   dead.

* LVI *

TAKE REFUGE in the shadow of the guide that you may escape from the enemy that opposes in secret.

Soul receives from soul that knowledge, therefore, not by book or from tongue. If knowledge of love's mysteries comes after emptiness of mind, that is illumination of heart.

* LVII *

SPIRITUAL mastery could very nearly have ceased to be manifested for lack of those whose heart is

45

quickened by an ardent desire to follow it. But the divine Wisdom never runs dry.

One of the effects of the divine bounty, grace and generosity, is that one finds the Master who can grant spiritual education. Without divine grace no one would find or recognize him.

Soon after I had found my master . . . he authorized me to initiate a certain man of letters who had been one of my teachers in Quranic reading. This man, following my example, wanted to become a disciple of my own master and kept on asking me to obtain permission for him to do so.

When I spoke to my master about it, he answered: Take him by the hand yourself since it is through you that he came to know about me. So I transmitted the teaching I myself had received and it bore fruit, thanks to the blessing inherent in my noble master's authorization.

However, since I had to leave Fez in order to go back to the Abu Zarwal tribe where I had left my parents, I was separated from him.

As for my master, he was still living in Fez al-Bali, and when I was about to set out on my journey to the tribe in question, I said to him: 'Where I am going there is no one at all with whom I could have spiritual conversation, and yet I am in need of such exchange.'

He answered: 'Beget the man you need!' As though

46

he thought that spiritual generation could take place through me, or as though he already saw it. I spoke to him again on the same theme and again he replied: 'Beget them!'

Now, thanks to the blessing emanating from his authorization and from his secret, a man came to me (may God multiply his like in Islam) who, at the instant I saw him and he me, was filled by God to overflowing, to such a degree that he attained in one leap the spiritual station of self-transcendence and of subsisting in God. God is our warrant for what we say. In this very event, the virtue and secret power contained in authorization were revealed to me and all doubts or suggestions left me. Thanks and praise be to God.

⋆ LVIII ⋆

LET not thy heart
Rely, like others, on thine own virtue and piety.
Come under the shadow of the man . . .
Who enjoys close proximity to God.
Turn not away from obedience to him in any wise . . .
He is the sun of the spirit, not of the sky . . .
Out of all the forms of religious service
Choose thou the shadow of that dear friend of God . . .
Having chosen thy director, be submissive to him,
Even as Moses submitted to the commands of Khidr.
A friend is needed: travel not the road alone.
Take not thine own way through the desert . . .
Having chosen thy director, be not weak of heart,

Nor yet sluggish and lax as water and mud.
If thou takest umbrage at every rub
How wilt thou become a polished mirror?

⋆ LIX ⋆

MANSUR THE SPINNER, who   He dived into the sea
Declared: I am the True,   Of his non-entity
He swept the dust of God   And won for you and me
From every road he trod.   This pearl: I am the True!

⋆ LX ⋆

FOR THIRTY YEARS I sought God. But when I looked
carefully, I saw that in reality God was the Seeker and
I was the sought.

⋆ LXI ⋆

Lo! there were two factions contending together and
he said: O my people, why do you hasten after the
evil rather than the good? Why do you not ask forgiveness of God, that haply you might find mercy?
(Surah 27.45–6)

Do NOT take the side of those who betray their trust.
Seek God's forgiveness. Surely God is forgiving and
merciful. You shall not plead the cause of those who
betray themselves.   (Surah 4.105–7)

⋆ LXII ⋆

OUR MASTER used to say: The true way to hurt the
enemy is to be occupied with the love of the Friend.

On the other hand, if you engage in war with the enemy, he will have obtained what he wanted from you and at the same time you will have lost the opportunity of loving the Friend.

Whenever someone shows hostility towards you, whether he be one of you or not, do not be concerned with yourselves, but with what your Lord has commanded. Provided you do not defend yourselves, God will defend you and take care of your cause. But if you do defend yourselves and are concerned with your cause, He will leave it to you to manage it, and you will be powerless. For it is 'God who has power over all things'.

LXIII

THE more he strives to injure me
The greater is my clemency.

LXIV

WOULD you know what the step is! It is the freeing of the slave, or giving food in the hungry day to an orphan near of kin, or to some needy soul in his distress. Such are believers indeed. Patience and mercy are their counsel, their counsel to each other.

(Surah 90.11–17)

LXV

I SAID: 'God is greater!' I saw that all corrupt thoughts, and every thought but the thought of God, all were put to rout. The idea occurred to me that until a certain form enters the mind, sincerity of worship does not appear: until the word 'God' is uttered, there is no turning from corruption to wellbeing. Until I conceive the image of God's attributes, and gaze upon the attributes of the creature, ecstasy and tenderness and true adoration do not manifest themselves . . .

God, it seems, has made the declaration of His Unity to be the means of the cutting off of all hesitations, whereas He has made the ascription of partners to Him to be the cause of bewilderment . . .

Beholding this, I said: Come, let me efface from my gaze all that is perishing and vincible, that, when I look, I may be able to see only the Victor, the Eternal. I desire that, as much as I efface, my gaze may become fixed on God's attributes as Victor and Eternal and the true perfection of God. As much as I effaced I found myself to be the prisoner of things vincible, things created in time. It was as if God was turning about the things created in time: and in the midst of this I saw that I was upon God's shoulder. I looked again, and saw that not only I, but heaven too, and the skies, earth and the empyrean, all were upon God's shoulder. Whither would He cast us?

★ LXVI ★

INTUITION is generally given only to him whose heart is pierced by an intense longing and a strong desire to contemplate the Essence of His Lord. Intuitions of the divine Essence flow into such a man until he is extinguished in that Essence and thus freed from the illusion of any other reality. For this is the direction in which the divine Essence leads those whose gaze is continually upon it.

⋆ LXVII ⋆

O INDESTRUCTIBLE LOVE, O divine Minstrel,
We are pieces of steel and Thy Love is the magnet.

⋆ LXVIII ⋆

I SEEK Thee because of Thee, to seek nothing from Thee.

⋆ LXIX ⋆

O THOU who art the sufficiency of those who seek of Thee to be sufficed.

O Thou who seekest him that desires Thee: O Thou desire of him who seeks Thee.

O Thou cry of those who cry for help.

O Thou focus of me in my distractedness.

O Thou of the two hands in mercy stretched.

O Thou power of the powerless, Thou glory of the worthless.

O Thou guide of the perplexed, security of the trusting, and desire of the yearning.

O Thou before whose greatness all things are humbled, whose command the heavens obey.

O Thou refuge of every outcast, friend of every lonely soul, covenant-keeping, secret-knowing, Lord of majesty and power.

O Thou whose beauty no thoughts can encompass, whose perfection no vision can conceive.

★ LXX ★

O MY GOD, how gentle art Thou with him who has transgressed against Thee, how near Thou art to him who seeks Thee, how tender to him who petitions Thee, how kindly to him who hopes in Thee. By what is hidden of Thy Names and by what the veils conceal of Thy splendour, forgive this restless spirit, this anguished heart.

★ LXXI ★

GRANT US, O lord, in our coming and our going, in our staying, in the things we speak, and will, and ponder, to be immune from doubts and notions and illusions which shroud our hearts from exploring the hidden mysteries.

'THOU'—MY LORD—DESIRING

LXXII

HE CALLED OUT in the darkness: There is no god but
Thou. Praise be to Thee.   (Surah 21.87)

There is no god but He, the merciful Lord of mercy.
                                  (Surah 2.163)

Say: He is my Lord: there is no god but He. In Him
have I trusted and to Him do I turn.   (Surah 13.30)

Praise be to God, Lord of the worlds,
The merciful Lord of mercy.
Master of the judgement Day.

Thou our only worship, Thou our one recourse,
Guide us in the straight road,
The road of those whom Thou hast graced . . .
                                  (Surah 1.1–7)

Everything upon earth is transient: the face of thy
Lord abides.   (Surah 55.26)

Remember Me and I will remember you . . .
                                  (Surah 2.152)

Remember the Name of your Lord: devote yourself
wholly to Him. He is the Lord of the east and of the
west. There is no god save He: take Him for your
trust.   (Surah 73.8–9)

God's friends—surely unfearing and ungrieving.
                                  (Surah 10.62)

God well pleased with them and they well pleased
with Him.   (Surah 5.119

O soul, thou art at rest
abiding in the divine presence.   (Surah 89.27)

There is no secrecy around which men gather, but He
is their fourth, or of four but He is their fifth, or of
five but He is their sixth. Fewer or more, and wherever they be, He is among them.   (Surah 58.7)

Desiring the face of God.   (Surah 2.272)

* LXXIII *

How shall I hope in Thee, being the 'me' I am?
How shall I not hope in Thee, Thou being who Thou
    art?

* LXXIV *

IT SUFFICES me for honour that I should be Thy
servant: it suffices me for grace that Thou shouldst
be my Lord.

* LXXV *

O MY GOD, the petitioners stand before Thy gate and
the needy seek refuge in Thy courts. The ship of the
wretched stands on the shore of the ocean of Thy
goodness and thy grace, seeking passage into the
presence of Thy mercy and compassion.

* LXXVI *

O GOD, I call upon Thee by Thy majesty at its most
radiant, for every splendour of Thine is truly splendid.

O God, I call upon Thee by Thy entire glory, by Thy beauty at its most beautiful . . . all things suppliant unto Thee are beloved of Thee: so, O God, I call upon Thee by all things suppliant unto Thee. O God, I call upon Thee by that which Thou art, in power and in greatness, calling upon Thee by every several element of that power and majesty. I seek Thee thus, O God, in the name of that wherewith Thou answerest when I call upon Thee. Our desire is unto Thee, O God. Thine are the Names most excellent and the attributes most high. Thine is the supremacy, the glory and the grace.

★ LXXVII ★

I WAS a hidden treasure and desired to be known. So I created the creation in order that I might be known.

★ LXXVIII ★

O LORD, give me eyes
    Which see nothing but Thy glory.
Give me a mind that finds delight
    In Thy service.
Give me a soul
    Drunk in the wine of Thy wisdom.

O Lord, though the blue flower be poisonous,
    It is of Thy garden,
And if Abdallah be a sinner,
    He is of Thy people.

Lord, when Thou wert hidden from me,
   The fever of life possessed me:
When Thou revealest Thyself,
   This fever of life departeth.

O Lord, intoxicate me
   With the wine of Thy love.
Make me empty
   Of all but Thy love.

★ LXXIX ★

ONE CAME to the Beloved's door and knocked. And a voice from within whispered: 'Who is there?' And the lover answered saying: 'It is I.'

Then the voice said: 'There is no room in this house for thee and me.' And the door was not opened to him. So the lover went back into the desert and fasted and prayed. At the end of a year, he returned once more to the Beloved's door and knocked.

And the voice from within said again: 'Who is there?' This time, the lover, having learned self-renunciation, answered: 'It is thyself.' And the door was opened.

★ LXXX ★

In THY perfect light   Veiled, Thy image fair
Loverhood I learn,   Dances in my heart
To Thy beauty bright   Which, beholding there,
Line and rhyme to turn.   I have learned this art.

PRAISE be to God Who alone is exalted in power and abidingness and praise, the One, the only, the ever subsisting, Who has curtained us with His grace, Who gazes into all our secret and our open ways, the King Who bestows and withholds, Who binds and breaks, in Whom is wealth and weal, uttering the ancient word, the ever abiding, Whose praise is in the thunder and the rain, in the stars and the trees, in powers and men, in sun and moon. He sets His trace in every thing. On every tongue of meaning He has opened secret things to minds that comprehend and hear the praise of all beings and see grace in every handiwork.

He has inspired us with the knowledge of His being and made us yearn for His righteousness. His being has aroused our desire. How shall the hearts of His lovers not be breached with ardour to find Him, their souls not be bewildered with awe and with sad fear lest He withdraw afar from them? How shall their spirits be at rest when He has called them to the highest station and the wealthiest state and the most lightsome honour?

Hearts find no rest except in the recollection of Him, in His praise. Nowhere can they recline, save on the carpet of His good pleasure on the day they find Him.

✲ LXXXII ✲

Ne'er from my nostrils went
Thy sweet familiar scent,
Ne'er vanished from my sight
Thine image bright.

So deep have I tasted
The infinite cup of love,
That till all time and age
Love's fires in my heart rage.

✲ LXXXIII ✲

I die, and yet not dies in me
The ardour of my love for Thee,
Nor hath Thy love, mine only goal,
Assuaged the fever of my soul.

To Thee alone my spirit cries,
In Thee my whole ambition lies,
And still Thy wealth is far above
The poverty of my poor love.

I turn to Thee in my request
And seek in Thee my final rest:
To Thee my loud lament is brought,
Thou dwellest in my secret thought.

To Thee alone is manifest
The heavy labour of my breast,
Else never kin or neighbours know
The brimming measure of my woe.

Guidest Thou not upon this road
The rider weaned of his load,
Delivering from the steeps of death
The traveller as he wandereth?

O then to me Thy favour give
That, so attended, I may live,
And overwhelm with ease from Thee
The rigour of my poverty.

⋆ LXXXIV ⋆

LOVE IS where the glory falls
Of Thy face on convent walls,
Or on tavern walls, the same
Inextinguishable flame.

Nay, what is more, it is the 'Truth' who is Himself
At once the Lover and the Beloved,
The seeker and the sought.
He is loved and sought in His character
As 'the One who is All',
And He is the lover and seeker when viewed
As the sum of all particulars and plurality.

⋆ LXXXV ⋆

I WAS SAYING: God, . . . this gaze of mine goes unto
Thee and to Thy bounty and follows after Thee. I
quickly efface that thought and return to the Thou-
ness of God. Similarly, whatever of the attributes of
God come into my mind, I quickly efface them and
return to the Thou-ness of God. I say: If God's

Thou-ness were not, my entity would not be . . . Since my entity and my qualities and my state of being and my breath of being all exist in Thee, and in Thee again are effaced, therefore, Thou, God, art my First and my Last. . . .

The clue to saying 'God' is to forget 'I-ness' and to remember the Thou-ness of God. So I say: 'God,' that is: Thou, God, art my hearing and my sight, my reason and my spirit, my heart and my perception. Why should I think upon the imperfection or perfection of these things? The conclusion is that it is necessary to become estranged from all these things and to belong exclusively to the Thou-ness of God, living or dead, in sickness or in health.

Now I gaze constantly at my perception to see how God converts it. I said: 'O God, keep firm in my perception the rules of worship and sincere service, of standing and bowing and prostrating, and of trembling in awe and keep my perception concentrated.' Then suddenly, I become distraught of God and depart from place to no-place, from contingencies to the non-contingent, from creature to the Creator, from self to selflessness: and I see that all the kingdoms belong to the sum of my perceptions. . . .

God inspired me saying: 'I gave thou-ness to thee for this purpose that when thou becomest distraught in Me, and thy heart is weary of my nearness, thou mayest gaze upon thyself and become busy with thyself.'

LODGERS WE, who on Thy threshold dwell
And nightingales that in Thy garden sing,
Whether we leave Thy door, or waiting, stand,
Of only Thee we speak, of Thee we hear.
Since we are captives caught within Thy nets,
Where shall we thrust our passion or our heads?
And since in Thy affection we draw breath,
How shall we yearn for strangers? Lo! we lay
Our heads upon the threshold at Thy door
Waiting to come to Thee. Since we have quaffed
The beaker of Thy love, we yield our hearts
And make our lives Thy ransom: since we come
Again into Thy street, we turn our backs
On all that is, save Thee. Our souls are bound
To serve Thee, though in grief, and we have died
To selfhood! We are captives of Thy love
And have not strength to flee. Thy beauty's fever
Hath lit a flame. Shall not our hearts be burned?

OTHERS staked their fortune on ease
And would not take up the burden of love.
We Thy lovers, were the ones whose hearts,
    experienced
In grief, staked all on grief, and took up the burden
    of love.
He, God, looked forth and beheld His own form in
    the world,
In the person of Adam.

He pitched His tent in the field of Adam's body
Which He had formed of water and clay.
Hafiz wrote in his joy-book of Love for Thee
On the day when his pen renounced all desire
For the goods of this world and renounced happiness
In what the world can offer.

★ LXXXVIII ★

QUESTION: According to Muslim belief, it is blasphemous for the dervishes to say: We do not fear Hell nor covet Heaven.

Answer: They do not mean this. They mean that fear and covetousness are not the paths in which a man should be reared.

★ LXXXIX ★

O GOD, Thou knowest that paradise weighs not with me so much as the wings of a gnat. If Thou befriendest me by Thy recollection and sustaineth me with Thy love and makest it easy for me to obey Thee, then give Thou paradise to whosoever Thou wilt.

★ XC ★

TWO WAYS I love Thee—selfishly,
And next, as worthy is of Thee.
'Tis selfish love that I do nought
Save think on Thee with every thought:
'Tis purest love when Thou dost raise
The veil to my adoring gaze.

★ XCI ★

THE TRUE mosque in a pure and lowly heart is builded:
there let all men worship God.

★ XCII ★

IN POVERTY I sought her, yet was rich
In having poverty my attribute.
Wherefore I cast away impoverishment
Alike and riches. When to jettison
My poverty and wealth assured to me
The merit of my quest, I thrust aside
My merit also: and therein appeared
Evident my good fortune—she who would
Reward me (and naught else) became my prize.

★ XCIII ★

HE MAKETH me desire
From self to leap,
My soul, free and entire
For Him to keep.

The stations upon the
way
Imprisoned me:
For Him I will break
away
From my bonds and be
free.

★ XCIV ★

IF THOU hast ears to hear,
Receive my message clear;
With Him to link thy heart,
Thou must from self depart.

Be silent, where the sight
Perceive the vision bright:
What speech must else declare
Is all beholding there.

Except a man himself deny,
To self he shall not wholly die,
Nor realize the mystery
Of unity.

⋆ XCV ⋆

THE LOVER joys to dwell
In love with love:
Yet some, as strange I tell,
Do Love reprove.
About God's love I hover
While I have breath,
To be His perfect lover,
Until my death.

⋆ XCVI ⋆

UNTO THEE are we come, by Thine own bringing, where none but Thee suffices us. There is welcome at Thy door and honour in Thy courtyard. Grace at Thy door is the lot of the needy. Though sin has alienated me from Thee, Thou rulest my heart irreplaceably. Drowning, Thou knowest all that is in me. Take the hand of Thy drowning one, trusting in Thee.

★ XCVII ★

WHEN she had prayed the evening prayer, she said:
O my God, in kings' palaces the doors are closed, the
curtains drawn. Every lover is alone with his beloved.
Here is my station, between Thy hands.

★ XCVIII ★

THE PIOUS sheikh may promise future bliss,
Disciple of the taverner-priest among I.
He brings me where joy is!

What drunkenness is this that brings me hope?
Who was the cup bearer and whence the wine?
That minstrel singing with full voice divine
What lay was his? For 'mid the woven rope
Of song he brought word from my Friend to me,
Set to his melody.

★ XCIX ★

THE WINE of God's grace hath no brim:
If it appears to have a brim, 'tis the fault of the Cup.

★ C ★

DRINK of this Presence. Be not thou a jar
Laden with water and its lip stone dry!

★ CI ★

THIN is the glass and clear is the wine:
The two are alike in mutual resemblance.
It is as if there were only wine and no glass at all,
Or as if only glass and no wine there.

GOD is the light of the heavens and the earth.
The likeness of His light is as a niche
Wherein is a lamp.
The lamp is in a glass, and the glass, as it were,
A star for brilliance.
The lamp is kindled from a blessed tree,
An olive neither of the east nor of the west,
The oil of which is almost incandescent
Of itself, without the touch of fire.

Light upon light.

God guides to His light whom He wills.

God affords these striking similitudes
On men's behalf,
And He has knowledge of everything.

This in the houses God has allowed should be
established in which His Name should be remembered,
and wherein, glorifying Him by morning and by
evening, are men whom neither trading nor merch-
andising divert from the remembrance of God, the
performance of the prayer rite and the bringing of
alms—all in awe of a day when hearts and eyes alike
will be in consternation.   (Surah 24.35–7)

TAUGHT by desire to wake through night's long hours
Mine eye hath won to see Thee while it sleeps not.
O happy, happy, night, in which Thy vision

I hunted after with my net of waking!
The full moon, being Thy copy, represented
To my unslumbering eye Thy face's image . . .
Thus Abraham of old, the Friend of Allah,
Upturned his eye, what time he scanned the heavens.
Now is the pitchy gloom for us made dazzling,
Since Thou Thy splendour gav'st me for my
    guidance.
When Thou from mine eye in outward seeming
Art gone, I cast it inward, there to find Thee.

★ CIV ★

HE LIES and perjures all that's true
Who swears he is in love with two.
The heart has not sufficient place
To hold two loves in one embrace,
Nor may the second love affair
Claim with the first an equal share.

For as the reason is unique,
It cannot know, though it may seek,
Another power to create
Beside the all Compassionate.

And so the heart's that likewise one
Is constituted to love none
Except that single darling dear
Be he afar or be he near.
The man who claims a dual role
Is thus, as these examples prove,
A doubtful follower of love's laws,
And traitor to religion's cause.

And by that self same reasoning,
True faith is too a single thing.
He who a second serves as well
Condemns himself an infidel.

★ CV ★

In His love the heart hath life.
Longing for Him the soul hath victory . . .

Beware! say not: He is all beautiful
And we His lovers. Thou art but the glass
And He the face confronting it, which casts
Its image in the mirror. He alone
Is manifest and thou in truth art hid.

Pure love, like beauty, coming but from Him,
Reveals itself in thee. If, steadfastly,
Thou canst regard, thou wilt at length perceive
He is the mirror also, He alike
The treasure and the casket. 'I' and 'Thou'
Have here no place, and are but fantasies
Vain and unreal.

★ CVI ★

THE BREATH of our praise steals the soul away little by
little from being prisoner in this world. Our breaths
soar up with choice words, as a gift from us to the
abode of everlastingness.

Then comes to us the recompense of our praise, a
recompense from God the merciful. For then He
causes us to seek more good works, so that His servant
may win more of His mercy. Verily the source of our
delight in prayer is the divine Love which without
rest draws the soul home.

Thus it is that the souls of those who have known

God seek after the green meadows, the beautiful vistas, the fresh green gardens. Yet all those things that they long for, echoing their experience of God, are a source also of pain for them, because they serve only to remind them. . . . They recall the lost Beloved. Sad indeed is then their lot.

After their union with Him, God separates them again from Himself and grants them their individuality again. Then He makes them absent from this world when they are in union with Him and makes them again present in this world when He has separated them from Himself. Thus it is that their absence from the world is but a facet of their presence with God and their presence in this world is a necessary cause of their absence from God. . . .

The Sufi is himself after he has not been truly himself (in ecstasy). He is present in Himself and in God, after having been present in God and absent in himself. This is . . . so that he can put everything in its right place and assess it correctly. Once more he assumes his individual attributes. His personal qualities persist in him. Thus his actions in the world, when he has reached the zenith of spiritual achievement vouchsafed by God, become a pattern for his fellow men.

The soul grieves then, and becomes used to its normal state, because it has lost its prime perfection. . . . Its regret is profound and its anguish for what it has lost continues in its conscious existence and its

conscious reality. . . . Its needs have returned to it.
How should it not suffer for being banished from God?
The soul was satisfied and now thirsts anew.

★ CVII ★

No! No! He said to me: Thou art neither near, nor
far, neither absent nor present, neither alive nor dead.
So listen to my testament: when I name thee, do not
name thyself; and when I adorn thee, do not adorn
thyself. And do not recollect Me. For if thou recol-
lectest Me, I shall cause thee to forget my recollection.

And He unveiled to me the face of every living
thing and I saw it attaching itself to his Face. Then
He unveiled to me the back of every living thing,
and I saw it attaching itself to his Command and
Prohibition.

And He said to me: Look upon my Face. And I
looked, and He said: There is naught beside Me. And
I said: There is naught beside Thee. And He said to
me: Look upon thy face. And I looked, and He said:
There is naught beside thee. And I said: There is
naught beside me. And he said: Depart, for thou hast
learned.

★ CVIII ★

Love is a fire, whose spark within the heart
Consumes the veil of every accident:
When intricate desire is wholly burned,
Naught else abiding, love alone abides.

★ CIX ★

ALL THIS TALK and turmoil and noise and movement
is outside of the veil. Within the veil is silence and
calm and rest. Dost thou hear how there comes a voice
from the brooks of running water? But when they
reach the sea they are quiet, and the sea is neither
augmented by their incoming nor diminished by their
outgoing.

★ CX ★

O THOU whose sacred precincts none may see,
Unseen Thou makest all things seen to be:
Thou and we are not separate, yet still
Thou hast no need of us, but we of Thee.

None by endeavour can behold Thy face,
Or access gain without prevenient grace:
For every man some substitute is found,
Thou hast no peer and none can take Thy place.

Of accident and substance Thou hast nought,
Without constraint of cause Thy grace is wrought:
Thou canst replace what's lost, but if Thou'rt lost,
In vain a substitute for Thee is sought.

In me Thy beauty, love and longing wrought:
Did I not seek Thee, how would'st Thou be sought?
My love is as a mirror in the which
Thy beauty into evidence is brought.

O Lord, none but Thyself can fathom Thee.
Yet every mosque and church doth harbour Thee:
I know the seekers and what 'tis they seek
Seekers and sought are all comprised in Thee.

★ CXI ★

FLY . . . to the desert,
There by so remote a fountain
That, whichever way one travelled
League on league, one yet should never,
Never, meet the face of man—
There to pitch my tent for ever,
There to gaze on my Beloved:
Gaze, till gazing out of gazing,
Grow to being her I gaze on,
She and I no more, but in one
Undivided being blended.
All that is not One must ever
Suffer with the wound of absence.
And whoever in Love's city
Enters, finds but room for One,
And but in Oneness Union.

★ CXII ★

Now I have known, O Lord,
What lies within my heart:
In secret, from the world apart,
My tongue has talked with my Adored.

So, in a manner, We
United are, and one:
Yet, otherwise, disunion
Is our estate eternally.

73

Though from my gaze profound
Deep awe has hid Thy face,
In wondrous and ecstatic grace
I feel Thee touch my inmost ground.

★ CXIII ★

WHAT is to be done, O Muslims?
I do not recognize myself.
I am neither Christian, nor Jew, nor Gabr, nor Muslim.
I am not of the east, nor of the west, nor of the land,
nor of the sea:
I am not of nature's mint, nor of the circling heavens.
I am not of earth, nor of water, nor of air, nor of fire:
I am not of the empyrean, nor of the dust, nor of
existence, nor of entity.
I am not of India, nor of China, nor of Bulgar, nor of
Saqsin:
I am not of the kingdom of the two 'Iraqs, nor of the
country of Khurasan.
I am not of this world, nor of the next, nor of Paradise,
nor of Hell.
I am not of Adam, nor of Eve, nor of Eden and
Ridwan.
My place is the placeless, my trace is the traceless:
'Tis neither body, nor soul, for I belong to the Soul of
the Beloved.
I have put duality away, I have seen the two worlds
are one:
One I seek, One I know, One I see, One I call.

He is the First, He is the Last, He is the Outward, He
is the Inward . . .
I am intoxicated with love's cup: the two worlds have
passed out of my ken . . .

⋆ CXIV ⋆

I AM so entirely absorbed in You.
Of mine own existence nothing but the name remains,
Till it becomes one We, it is two separate 'I's.

⋆ CXV ⋆

REASON, explaining love, can nought but flounder,
Like ass in mire: love is Love's own expounder.
Does not the sun himself the sun declare?
Behold him! All the proof thou seekest is there.

⋆ CXVI ⋆

HOW SHALL I say that existence is mine, when I have
no knowledge of myself, or how that I exist when
mine eyes are fixed upon Him?

⋆ CXVII ⋆

I WAS snow and melted away, so that the earth drank
me up,
Till I became one mist of soul and mounted to the sky.

⋆ CXVIII ⋆

OUR journey is to the rose garden of union.
Life is the vessels, union the clear draught in them,
Conceive the Soul as a fountain

And these created things as rivers:
While the fountain flows, the rivers run from it . . .
In the world of divine Unity is no room for number.

From this world of severance to that world of
    union. . . .
When Thou art hidden, I am of the infidels,
When Thou art manifest, I am of the faithful. . . .
Pour out wine till I become a wanderer from myself:
For in selfhood and existence
I have felt only weariness.

⋆ CXIX ⋆

IF THE voice of God were heard speaking unto Moses
from an acacia bush and saying: 'I am'; how should
He not speak with the tongue of His friend, the soul
of man?

⋆ CXX ⋆

THE SAYING: 'I am the Real', was lawful for the bush.
Why is it not lawful in the mouth of a good man?

Every man whose heart is pure from doubt
Knows of a surety that there is no being but One.
Saying: I am, belongs only to the truth. . . .

The glory of the truth admits no duality,
In that glory is no 'I' or 'We' or 'Thou'.

'I', 'Thou', 'We' 'He' are all one thing,
For in unity there is no distinction of persons.

Every man who, as a void, is empty of self
Re-echoes within him the cry: 'I am the Real'.
Travelling, travel and traveller, all become one.
Incarnation and communion spring from 'other',
But from the mystic journey comes very unity.

* CXXI *

A MAN may know this mystery when he passes forth
From the part and travels to the whole.
Of what sort is this traveller?
Who is this wayfarer?
It is he who is acquainted with his own origin.
He is a traveller who passes on with haste,
And becomes pure from self as fire from smoke.
His journey is a progress of revelation from the
    contingent
To the necessary, leading away from darkness and
    defect.
He travels back his first journey, stage by stage,
Till he attains the being of the perfect man.

* CXXII *

PURE BEING, singing of love unto itself in a perfect
harmony.

* CXXIII *

WHEN TRUTH its light doth show,
I lose myself in reverence
And am as one who never travelled thence
To life below.

When I am absented
From self to Him, and Him attain,
Attainment's self thereafter proveth vain,
And self is dead.

In union divine
With Him, Him only do I see.
I dwell alone and that felicity
No more is mine.

This mystic union
From self hath separated me:
Now witness concentration's mystery
Of two made one.

⋆ CXXIV ⋆

My being was effaced
In my beholding, and I was detached
From by beholding's being . . .

⋆ CXXV ⋆

Said I: To whom belongs Thy beauty?
He replied: Since I alone exist in Me,
Lover, Beloved and Love am I in one
Beauty and mirror, and the eyes that see . . .

Affirm God's being and deny thine own
This is the meaning of 'No god but He'.

When me at length Thy love's embrace shall claim
To glance at paradise I'd deem it shame,
While to a Thee-less Heaven were I called,
Such heaven and hell to me would seem the same.

FROM the unmanifest I came and pitched my tent in the forest of material substance. I passed through mineral and vegetable kingdoms. Then my mental equipment carried me into the animal kingdom. Having reached there, I crossed beyond it. Then in the crystal-clear shell of the human heart, I nursed the drop of self into a pearl and, in association with good men, wandered round the Prayer House and, having experienced that, crossed beyond it. Then I took the road that leads to Him and became a slave at His gate. Then the duality disappeared and I became absorbed in Him.

As WATER, lifted from the deep again,
Falls back in individual drops of rain
Then melts into the universal main.
All you have been, and seen, and done, and thought.
Not you, but I have seen and been and wrought.

Now STANDS no more between the Truth and me,
    Or reasoned demonstration,
    Or proof, or revelation.
Now, brightly shining forth, Truth's luminary
    Has driven out of sight
    Each flickering, lesser light.

He only knoweth God, whom God hath shown
　　Himself. Shall the eternal
　　Be known of the diurnal?
Not in His handiwork may God be known.
　　Can endless time be pent
　　Into a chance event?
Of Him, through Him, and unto Him, a sign
　　Of truth, an attestation
　　He grants through inspiration.
Of Him, through Him, His own, a truth divine,
　　A knowledge proved and sure
　　Hath made our hearts secure.

★ CXXIX ★

LOVE is a quality of the Creator.
Lover, and love, and beauty—three, yet One
Creator and sustainer, only God . . .
In perfect loveliness He was revealed,
Giving to spiritual men the power
Of love. His manifesting attributes
Found housing in the lover; power from Power,
Knowledge from Knowledge, hearing from Hearing,
Sight from Sight, speech from Speech divine informed:
Will grew from Will, and life from Life was born,
Beauty from Beauty glowed, continuance
Of love in His continuance increased,
In man's affection God's affection shone,
And of His love revealing, man's love sprang.
Since in these attributes man knows the Friend,
Seeing himself, he doth the Friend behold:

So, secretly, he doth His Name proclaim;
I have no other in my cloak but God.
When man strips off the cloak, he doth escape.
Strip off that cloak which serves but as a house.
Now sign the document of fellowship
And chant the formula of severance:
When thou transcendeth: 'Glory be to God',
Wipe off the dust of selfhood from thy soul.

✶ CXXX ✶

THE WORLD is God's pure mirror clear
To eyes when free from clouds within.
With Love's own eyes the mirror view
And there see God to Self akin.
Then praise Him, Soul, enflamed with Love
As larks in dawn new songs begin.

✶ CXXXI ✶

I THOUGHT I had arrived at the very Throne of God
and said to it: 'O Throne, they tell us that God rests
upon thee.' 'O Bayazid,' replied the Throne, 'we are
told here that He dwells in a humble heart.'

✶ CXXXII ✶

WHERE are you going, O Bayazid?
Where will you bring your caravan to a halt?
Bayazid replied: At dawn I start for the Ka'bah!
Quoth the sage: What provision for the way have you?
He answered: I have two hundred silver dirhams.
See them tied up tightly in the corner of my cloak.

The sage said: Circumambulate me seven times.
Count this better than circumambulating the Ka'bah.
And, as for the dirhams, give them to me, O liberal
  one,
Know that you have finished your course
And obtained your wish.
You have made the pilgrimage
And gained the life to come.
You have become pure and that in a moment of time.
Of a truth that is God which your soul sees in me.
For God has chosen me to be His house.
Though the Ka'bah is the house of His grace and
  favours
Yet my body, too, is the house of His secrets.

Since He made *that* house, He has never entered it:
This house none but that living One enters.
When you have seen me, you have seen God
And have circumambulated the veritable Ka'bah.

To serve me is to worship and to praise God.
Think not that God is distinct from me.
Open clear eyes and look on me
That you may behold the light of God in a mortal.

The Beloved once called the Ka'bah 'My house',
But has said to me: 'O My servant', seventy times.

O Bayazid, you have found the Ka'bah
You have found a hundred precious blessings.

★ CXXXIII ★

IN MERCIFUL expansion I am all desire, whereby
The hopes of all who dwell upon My earth
Are wide expanded. But in terrible
Contraction, I am reverential awe
Entire, and whereso'er I turn mine eye
All things revere Me. Yet where these twain states
Unite, I am all nearness.

★ CXXXIV ★

FROM all eternity the Beloved unveiled this beauty
In the solitude of the unseen.
He held the mirror to His own face,
He displayed His loveliness to Himself.
He was both the spectacle and the spectator, no eye
But His had surveyed the universe.
All was one, there was no duality,
No pretence of 'mine' and 'thine'.

The vast orb of heaven with its myriad incomings
And outgoings, was concealed in a single point.
The creation lay cradled in the sleep of non existence,
Like a child 'ere it has breathed.
The love of the Beloved, seeing what was not,
Regarded non entity as existent.
Although He beheld His attributes and qualities
As a perfect whole in His own essence,
Yet He desired they should be displayed to Him
In another mirror,
And that each of His eternal attributes should become
Manifest accordingly in a diverse form.

Therefore, He created the verdant fields of time
And space and the life giving gardens of the world,
That every branch and leaf and fruit might show forth
His various perfections.
The cypress gave a hint of His comely stature
The rose gave tidings of His beauteous countenance.
Wherever beauty peeped out, love appeared beside it,
Whenever beauty shone in a rosy cheek,
Love lit his torch from the flame.

Whenever beauty dwelt in dark tresses, love came
And found a heart entangled in the coils.
Beauty and love are as body and soul, beauty is
The mine, and love the precious stone.
They have always been together from the very first.
Never have they travelled but in each other's company.

Man is the crown and final cause of the universe.
Though last in order of creation, man is first
In the process of divine thought.
For the essential part of him is the primal intelligence
Of universal reason which emanates immediately
From the Godhead.

'THOU LORD OF THE WORLDS'

O GOD, I never hearken to the voices of the beasts, or to the rustle of the trees, the splashing of the waters, the song of the birds, the whistling of the wind, or the rumbling of the thunder, but I sense in them a testimony to Thy unity and a proof of Thy incomparableness: that Thou art the all-pervading, the all-knowing, the all-wise, the all-just, the all-true, and in Thee is neither over-thought, nor ignorance, nor folly, nor injustice, nor lying.

O God, I acknowledge Thee in the proof of Thy handiwork and in the evidence of Thy doings. Grant me, O God, to seek Thy satisfaction with my satisfaction and the delight of a father in his child, remembering Thee in my love for Thee with serene tranquillity and firm resolve.

ONE DAY, in spring, her servant said to her: Come out and behold what God has made. But Rabi'ah answered: Come in and behold the Maker.

IT IS impossible to see our Lord while seeing anything other than Him, and all who have reached this degree of knowledge affirm the same. If the suggestions of imagination were to cease, you would contemplate the Eternal without ceasing.

He lies who claims to have drunk the wine of the initiates and to have understood their spiritual truths, yet does not detach himself from the world. . . . The paradise of knowledge is closed to him whose soul is not dead to the world, to the desire to act in it, to choose, to possess and to enjoy it—who is not dead to everything except God.

⋆ CXXXVIII ⋆

ONE DAY Majnun, whose love for Laila inspired many a Persian poet, was playing in a little sand heap, when a friend came to him and said: 'Why are you wasting your time in an occupation so childish?' 'I am seeking Laila in these sands,' replied Majnun.

His friend in amazement cried: 'Why? Laila is an angel, so what is the use of seeking her in the common earth?' 'I seek her everywhere,' said Majnun, bowing his head, 'that I may find her somewhere.'

⋆ CXXXIX ⋆

IF WE ARE beholding autumn or spring
Really we are witnessing the ways of the Beloved.
In the fair and ugly forms of the mundane
We see manifest the effulgence of God.
Our hearts are turned towards God
And eyes towards beloveds,
We are spectators of this lovely spring-like pageant.

REAL LOVE is born out of the love of beautiful forms. The lover devotes his whole attention to the beloved. This attention evokes reflection, due to which he concentrates on the beauty and the excellences of the beloved. This very thought leads him to the knowledge of the Being who has adorned his beloved with inward excellence and outward beauty. When this knowledge is attained by the lover, he comes to know that whatever perfection or beauty exists in the universe is due to the Beauty and Excellence of its Creator. It is personal to Him and for the universe it exists through Him alone.

* CXLI *

ALL BEAUTY will tomorrow belong to Thy Face alone, But today it is present in detail in the whole world.

* CXLII *

THEY intuit the absolute Beauty with their inward eyes, as they perceive the formal limited beauty with their external eyes.

* CXLIII *

DOES not the Qur'an say: Praising to God is all that is, in the heavens and in the earth. His is the kingdom and His the praise, for His is the authority over all things. He it is who has created you, and among you one is graceless and another believing. God is cognizant of your doings. With truth He created the heavens and the earth: He fashioned you and with beauty shaped you. Unto Him is the homecoming. (Surah 64.1–3)

★ CXLIV ★

THE WHOLE WORLD is the theatre of my Beloved
Wheresoever my mind opened its eyes,
They beheld the same Beloved.

★ CXLV ★

IN MY faith is comprised the love of the city and its inhabitants.

★ CXLVI ★

IF A scholar holds pen, paper and ink dear, it cannot be said that he is not a lover of learning. The Beloved in itself, should be only one, but love for other things, which are related to the Beloved, does not interfere with love of the Beloved. . . . Anything that one may love will be synonymous with loving His handiwork. So that the culmination of the stage of the lover and love is that all love is with God alone. . . . To hold anything dear as a means will not be considered 'partnership' in love and will not be considered a veil in the way to the real Beloved.

★ CXLVII ★

WHATEVER gold His seal
   may bear
Stamped at creation's
   compact there,
In whatsoever mint it be,
That gold belongs to me.

'Tis the love of Thee
Rocks the swelling sea,
Storm clouds in Thy
   train
Scatter pearls of rain.

BURDEN thy heart with love as thou likest. For, in reality, one loves the First Friend alone.

'GLORY be to Thee,' I cried. I gazed on the vision of God and on the wonders and purities of God. Having seen God with all His purities and wonders in the act of saying: 'Glory be to Thee', I then cried: 'Praise belongs to Thee'—that is, 'I desire to see the laudable qualities of God, and His beauties and graces, and I desire to gaze on all things lovely and good, that I may see God in the attribute of loveliness and goodness.'

And I saw that this beauty and this goodness of God were infinite: only I am seeing according to the measure of the trace, the greater the measure of the trace, the better I see. Even so I see God seated in all His attributes. I gaze again on the loci of the traces of each attribute of these realities, and see God in those traces, only I cannot tell the mode thereof. In prayer I cry 'God is greater'—that is, it is certified that He only is God, and upon whatsoever I gaze only Him I see. . . . 'Say: He is God, the One' (Surah 112.1), that is to say: 'O seeker, God is present, but thou art absent. Return out of that absence into his presence. For he is One and there is none other than He. . . .'

Every part of me became like to a bride reverencing her king in the privacy of the bridal chamber.

I said: 'O God, how blissful a state is love commingled with the reverence of Thee; very bliss it is.'

Thereafter, at dawn I gazed, to see how any man might behold the oneness of God. I saw that some men have seen God with an eye of poverty . . . some with the eye of form, some with the eye of direction, some with the eye of matter and temperament and the stars: and God is not without all these. I said: 'O God, sometimes I see Thee with the eye of one who likens; sometimes I see Thee with the eye of poverty and annihilation; sometimes with the eye of compulsion; sometimes with the eye of the passionate; sometimes with the eye of lovers. O God, to whomsoever Thou hast given an eye to see Thee, with whatever manner of constitution and temperament he has been endowed, inevitably his actions and motions have proceeded accordingly.'

Again, when I begin my recollection, I first of all do so on the basis of being absent from God. Then after that I perform my remembrance after the way of colloquy . . . saying: 'O God and Lord, this flesh and body of mine are the threshold of Thy door, wherein I have slept and squatted, I am before Thee, and I will not go from Thy presence to any other place. This body of mine, O God, is Thy workshop and my senses are engraved by Thee.'

'I have placed them before Thee: whatever Thou wilt do Thou engrave upon them, O God. I have come before Thee, for Thou art my Lord: whom

have I but Thee? If I depart hence, God, whither shall
I go? What place have I where I may alight and dwell?
For Thou art my Lord: I know no other to be my
Lord, but Thee.'

★ CL ★

THOUGH He be gone, mine every limb beholds Him
In every charm and grace of loveliness:
In music of the lute and flowing reed,
Mingled in consort with melodious airs,
And in green hollows where, in cool of eve,
Gazelles roam browsing, or at break of morn:
And where the gathered clouds let fall their rain
Upon a flowery carpet woven of blooms:
And where at dawn with softly trailing skirts
The zephyr brings to me his balm most sweet:
And when in kisses from the flagon's mouth
I suck wine dew beneath a pleasant shade.

★ CLI ★

NIGHT is with child, hast thou not heard men say?
Night is with child! what shall she bring to birth?
I sit and ask the stars when thou'rt away.
O come! and when the nightingale of mirth
Pipes in the spring awakened ground
In Hafiz' heart shall ring a sweeter sound,
Diviner nightingale's attune their lay.

★ CLII ★

BREATHES there one who can thank Him for even one
of His boons?

91

The subtle Inventor who on the floor of the earth
Painted a thousand forms of variegated colours.
The structure of the heavens and the rising of the stars
Are meant to teach a lesson to the wise.
He created the ocean, the earth, the trees and man.
He made the sun, the moon, the stars and days and
nights.
He drove the peg of mountains into the leathern floor
of earth,
And spread the floor of earth on the surface of water.
He turned the particles of dead earth by the light of
the sun,
Into orchards, gardens and beds of flowers.
The clouds quenched the thirst of the dried roots of
the trees
And attired the naked bough in the robes of spring.
The believer in Thy unity is not only man,
But every nightingale that warbles on the branch of a
tree.

★ CLIII ★

IF YOU contemplated Him in everything, contemplation of Him would veil all things from your sight.

If you contemplated Him, they would not hide
Him from you in the before and after and the time of
things.

★ CLIV ★

IN SOLITUDE where Being signless dwelt
And all the universe still dormant lay

92

Concealed in selflessness, One Being was,
Exempt from 'I' and 'Thou'-ness, and apart
From all duality: Beauty supreme,
Unmanifest, except unto Itself
By its own light, yet fraught with power to charm
The souls of all: concealed in the Unseen,
An Essence pure, unstained by aught of ill.

No mirror to reflect its loveliness . . .
   no eye had yet beheld its image.
To itself it sang of love in wordless measures. . . .

But beauty cannot brook concealment
And the veil, nor patient rest
Unseen and unadmired. 'Twill burst all bonds
And from its prison casement to the world
Reveal itself . . .
   . . . thou too, when some rare thought
Or beauteous image, or deep mystery
Flashes across thy soul, canst not endure
To let it pass, but holdst it: perchance
In speech or writing thou mayest send it forth
To charm the world. Whatever beauty dwells,
Such is its nature and its heritage
From everlasting Beauty, which emerged
From realms of purity to shine upon
The worlds and all the souls that dwell therein.

One gleam fell from it on the universe
And on the angels, and this single ray
Dazzled the angels till their senses whirled

Like the revolving sky. In diverse forms
Each mirror showed it forth, and everywhere
Its praise was chanted in new harmonies.

The cherubim, enraptured, sought for songs
Of praise. The spirits who explore the depths
Of boundless seas, wherein the heavens swim
Like some small boat, cried with one mighty voice:
Praise to the Lord of all the universe.

★ CLV ★

A SPRINKLING note of mirth
Cascades from heaven to earth,
O weary hearts be gay,
This is your day today.